ISBN-13: 978-1-4234-5114-3
ISBN-10: 1-4234-5114-7

Walt Disney Music Company
Wonderland Music Company, Inc.

DISTRIBUTED BY

HAL•LEONARD®
CORPORATION

7777 W. BLUEMOUND RD. P.O. BOX 13819 MILWAUKEE, WI 53213

In Australia Contact:
Hal Leonard Australia Pty. Ltd.
4 Lentara Court
Cheltenham, Victoria 3192 Australia
Email: ausadmin @ halleonard.com

Visit Hal Leonard Online at
www.halleonard.com

contents

Hannah Montana2

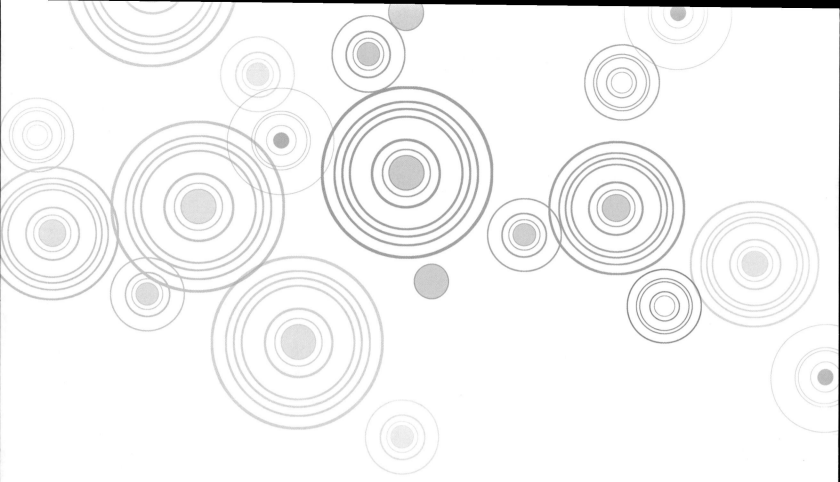

Meet Miley Cyrus

WE GOT THE PARTY

Words and Music by
KARA DioGUARDI

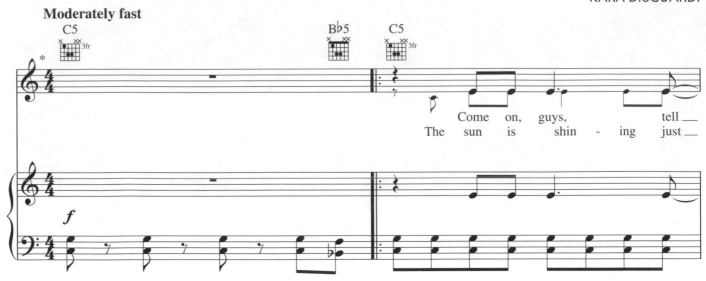

Come on, guys, tell_
The sun is shin - ing just_

_ me what we're do - ing. We're hang - in' 'round when we_
_ the way we like it. Let's get out of this hall -

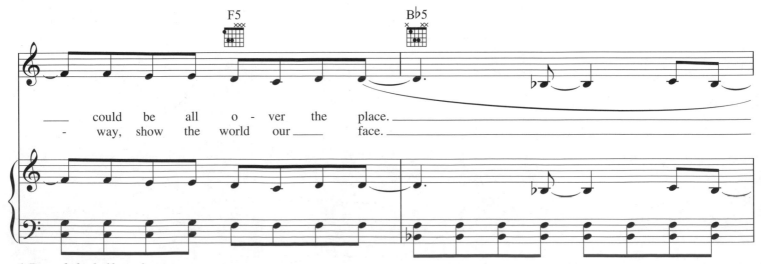

_ could be all o - ver the place.
- way, show the world our _ face. _

* Recorded a half step lower.

NOBODY'S PERFECT

Words and Music by MATTHEW GERRARD
and ROBBIE NEVIL

Moderately fast

Ev-'ry-bod-y makes mis - takes.

Ev-'ry-bod-y has those days.

One, two, three, four.

*Recorded a whole step lower.

MAKE SOME NOISE

Words and Music by ANDY DODD
and ADAM WATTS

I will be there with you all of the way. ___

Don't be a - fraid to be all that you are. ___

You'll be fine.

Don't let an - y - one ___ tell you that

you're not strong e - nough. _____

There's no one else who can stand in your ___ place, so come on, it's nev- er too ___ late. ___ May - be it's your time to lift off and fly. You won't know if you nev - er

D.S. al Coda

ROCK STAR

Words and Music by JEANNIE LURIE,
ARIS ARCHONTIS and CHEN NEEMAN

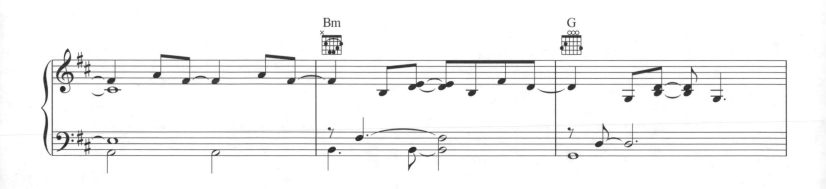

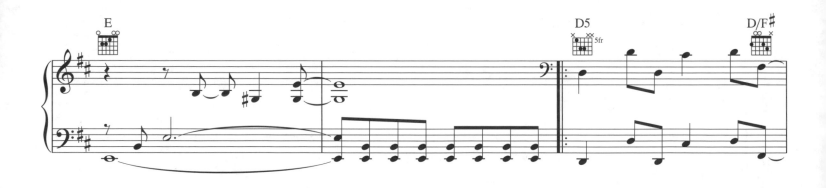

OLD BLUE JEANS

Words and Music by MICHAEL BRADFORD
and PAM SHEYNE

LIFE'S WHAT YOU MAKE IT

Words and Music by MATTHEW GERRARD
and ROBBIE NEVIL

Moderately fast

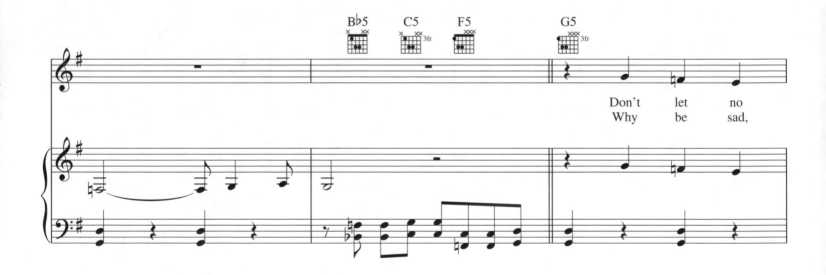

Don't let no
Why be sad,

small frus-tra-tion
bro-ken-heart-ed?

ev-er bring you down,___
There's so___ much to do,___

ONE IN A MILLION

Words and Music by TOBY GAD
and NEGIN DJAFARI

How did I get ___ here? I

turned a-round ___ and there ___ you were. ___ I did-n't think twice or ra-

*Recorded a half step higher.
**Melody is written an octave higher than sung.

To Coda

BIGGER THAN US

Words and Music by TIM JAMES
and ANTONINA ARMATO

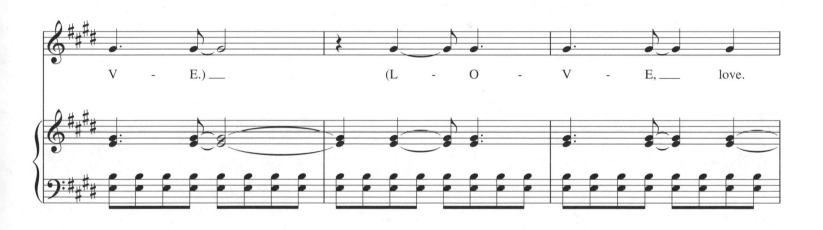

YOU AND ME TOGETHER

Words and Music by
JAMIE HOUSTON

Looks like we found ____ our - selves ____
An - y - one can have a day ____ when their

up a - gainst a wall, ____ in need of a lit -
heart is on ____ their sleeve. ____ No one wants to see

TRUE FRIEND

Words and Music by
JEANNIE LURIE

SEE YOU AGAIN

Words and Music by DESTINY HOPE CYRUS,
TIM JAMES and ANTONINA ARMATO

Moderately fast

I got my sights set on you,
I've got a way of know - ing
I got this cra - zy feel - ing

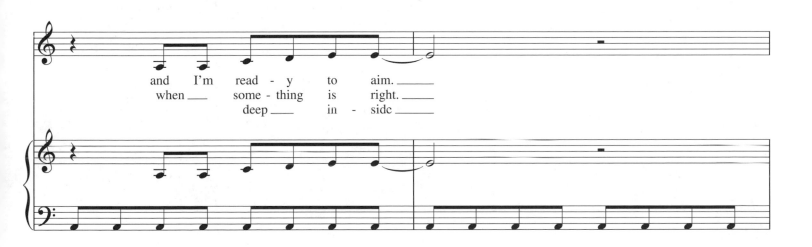

and I'm read - y to aim.
when some - thing is right.
deep in - side

I have a heart that will
I feel like I must have known
when you called and asked to see me

I got my sights set ___ on you, and I'm read-y to aim. ___ The last time, I freaked out; I just kept look-ing down. ___ I st-st-stut-tered when you

EAST NORTHUMBERLAND HIGH

Words and Music by SAMANTHA JO MOORE,
TIM JAMES and ANTONINA ARMATO

My prob-lem is not
Your prob-lem's not ___

-n't that ___ I miss ___ you, 'cause I don't. ___
___ for lack ___ of try - ing, 'cause you do. ___

My prob - lem is at ___
It's just that you're at ___

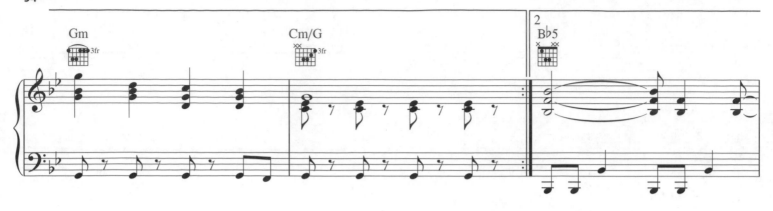

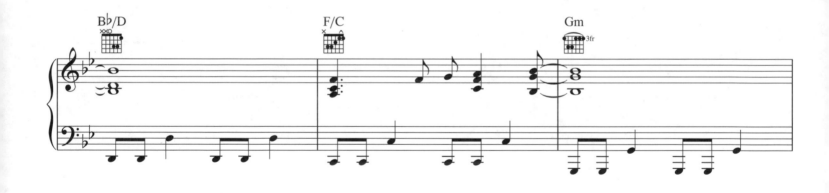

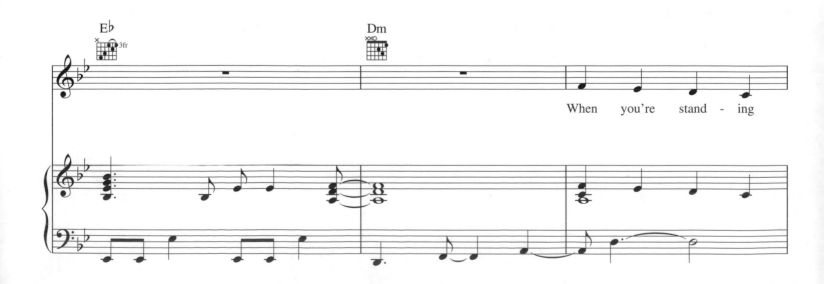

When you're stand - ing

LET'S DANCE

Words and Music by DESTINY HOPE CYRUS,
TIM JAMES and ANTONINA ARMATO

Melody is written an octave higher than sung.

Bbm7

dance: grab your girl-friends, grab your boy-friends, let it out. Let's

C7

dance. (Move_ your whole bod - y and let's_ start the par - ty.)
(Too much

Fm

1

rock for one girl can make_ her go cra - zy. I need some-one to dance_ with me, ba - by.)

2

(Dance!) The mu - sic's I need some-one to dance_ with me, ba - by.)

(Dance!)

When the night says hel - lo, yeah, get read -

- y to go. Turn it up, turn it loose, yeah, you've got _____ no ex - cuse. Just take _____

a chance, get out on the floor and dance.

Let's dance, what the week-end, what the night is all a-bout. Let's dance: grab your girl-friends, grab your boy-friends, let it out. Let's dance.

G.N.O.
(Girl's Night Out)

Words and Music by MATTHEW WILDER
and TAMARA DUNN

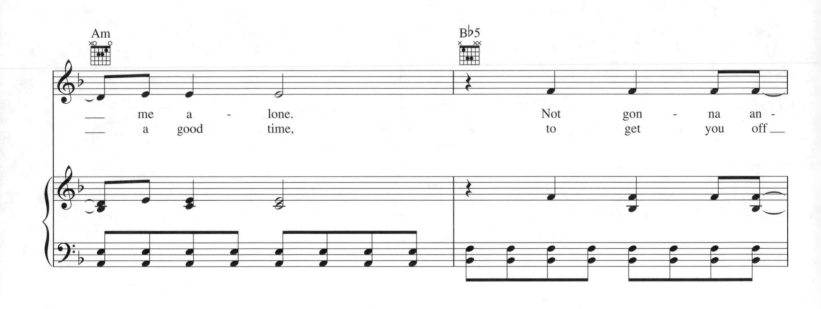

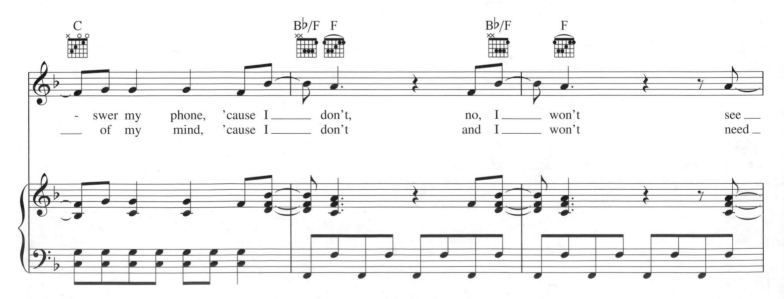

RIGHT HERE

Words and Music by DESTINY HOPE CYRUS,
TIM JAMES and ANTONINA ARMATO

AS I AM

Words and Music by DESTINY HOPE CYRUS,
ALEXANDER BARRY and SHELLY PEIKEN

Moderately fast

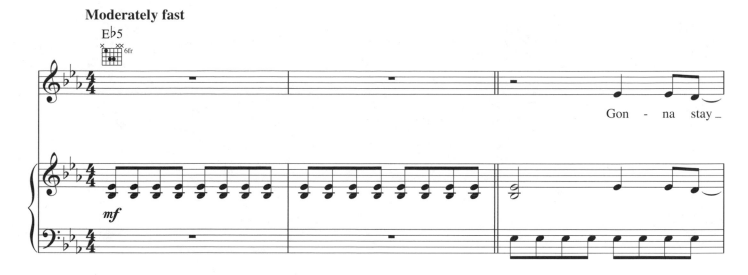

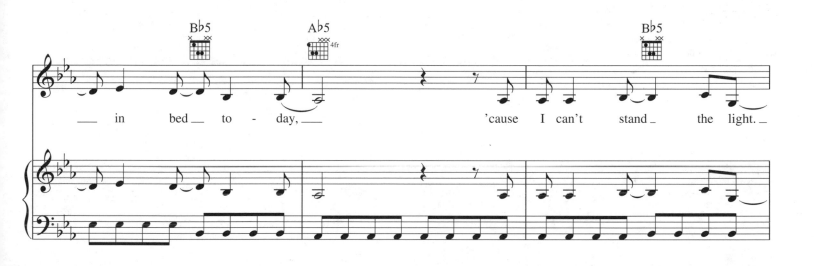

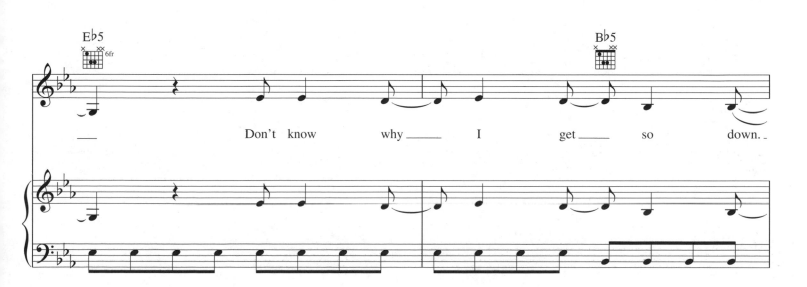

START ALL OVER

Words and Music by FEFE DOBSON,
SCOTT CUTLER and ANNE PREVIN

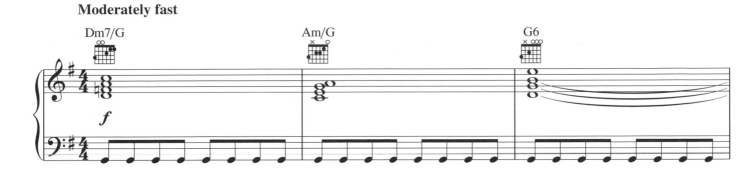

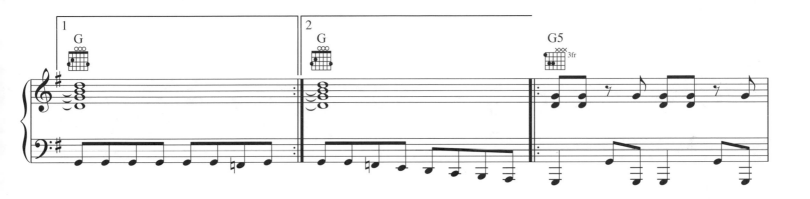

I have to won - der if _____ this wave's _

Fan - tas - tic and _____ ro - man - tic, all _____

Here I come, straight out of my mind, or worse, an - oth - er

chance to get burned _____ and start all o - ver.

I'm gon - na start all o - ver.

It's so eas-

CLEAR

Words and Music by DESTINY HOPE CYRUS,
ALEXANDER BARRY and SHELLY PEIKEN

GOOD AND BROKEN

Words and Music by DESTINY HOPE CYRUS,
TIM JAMES and ANTONINA ARMATO

Moderately fast

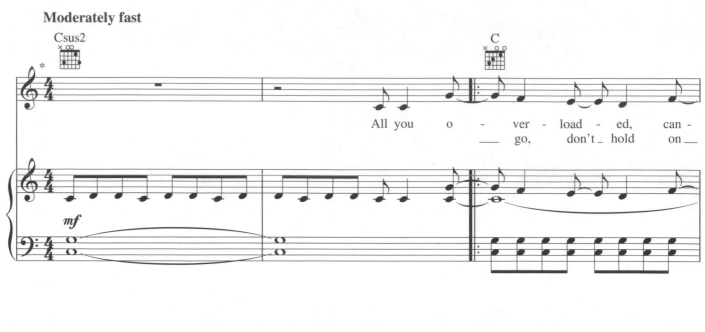

All you o - ver - load - ed, can- __ go, don't_ hold on

- dy coat - ed, your life's _____ im - plod - ing now.
__ to all _____ of _____ life's _____ hard - est parts. _

There's a risk _____ worth tak - ing, a pain _
When we think _____ of stop - ping, let's keep _

* *Recorded a half step lower.*

I MISS YOU

Words and Music by DESTINY HOPE CYRUS,
BRIAN GREEN and WENDI FOY GREEN

Lyrics:

I miss you; I miss your smile, and I still shed a tear ev'ry once in a while. And e-ven though it's dif-f'rent now, you're still here some-how. My heart won't let you go, and